Praise

SECOND ADO

"A roving, rhythmic, rebellious collection that puts the 'life' in 'third-life crisis,' *Second Adolescence* is both unflinching and forward-facing. Not a single confession, internal rhyme, or mote of inspiration goes unexplored in Rolnicki's verse as we follow the speaker on his journey of self-actualization, reveling in the hope that it is never too late - or too early - for a reinvention."

- T.S. Priest, writer @agirlcalledthomas

"*Second Adolescence* is hilarious, clever, and staggeringly honest about the realities of starting over. Rolnicki writes the kind of poetry that somehow makes you feel less alone."

- Caitlin Thomson, writer @cait.t.poetry

"Reading Joe's work is akin to taking a walk down meandering streets on a pleasant summer night. You don't go on this journey with an end goal in mind but for the surprising insights, funny observations, and oftentimes deliciously dark, endearing, and weirdly reassuring reflections that his words immerse you in."

- Akanksha Gupta, writer @madmedleys

"The only reason not to read *Second Adolescence* is if you are completely content with your perfectly procured life. Joe somehow brings worlds of words together in his own unique way—this compilation feels like the collected work of Chaucer, Dr. Seuss, and Alan Watts are having an orgy in your living room and you are deciding whether to watch or join in. A presentation on the nobility of hedonism at its finest.

- Abigail Lloyd, writer @neurodivergent.nightmare

"It is always refreshing to hear Joe's voice in my head; it speaks with a candor and sardonic profundity that is rare these days"

- Colin Tan, writer @juxtaproser

"*Second Adolescence* captures the nuances of transformation, ache and desire, all with a side of humor in Joe's well-known lyrical prose."

– Jennifer Walker, writer @everymileareward

"*Second Adolescence* tackles intense topics like nihilism and defying society's expectations with a flow reminiscent of nursery rhymes. The whimsical rhythm in contrast to the deep and sometimes dark content of the pieces creates a jarring yet addicting effect. This is a poetry book you won't want to put down."

– Brandi Batley, writer @writewithbrandi

"There is something about the way Joe plays with words, the way he imparts rhythm on the page - the blunt honesty in every poem. A collection at times lighthearted, and others poignant. *Second Adolescence* is the perfect title."

– Clementine Valerie Black, writer @clementinevalerieblack

"These revealing snapshots from a life examined will call to the 'that's me' in most of us. If he's 'The Fool', then maybe we all are."

– Lainey, writer @thelaineydayblog

"An honest, witty, and profound collection of poetry. Written with passion, fire, and a whole lot of heart."

– Emily Poetic, writer @em.poetic

"*Second Adolescence* is a visceral collection. It addresses those elements of growing up that few creative mediums acknowledge and reminds the reader that drifting is as much an art as conforming to a list of social norms."

– Ellie Sparks, writer @justtryingtobeoriginal

SECOND ADOLESCENCE

SECOND ADOLESCENCE

JOE
ROLNICKI

POEMS

atmosphere press

© 2022 Joe Rolnicki

Published by Atmosphere Press

Cover design by Senhor Tocas
Author photo by Sarah Uftring

No part of this book may be reproduced without permission from the author except in brief quotations and in reviews.

atmospherepress.com

TABLE OF CONTENTS

ONE: HOW TO STOP LYING

TWO: REPLACED

THREE: FREE TIME

For Father and Mother

ONE

HOW TO STOP LYING

I'M RUNNING OUT OF YEARS

I entered the suck today
I needed to journal today
Instead I looked at Instagram today
Instagram isn't the answer
Just like how sex wasn't the answer
Working harder wasn't the answer
Traveling farther wasn't the answer
Practicing gratitude wasn't the answer
Meditation wasn't the answer
Nostalgia wasn't the answer
Reading self-help wasn't the answer
Running marathons wasn't the answer
Losing weight wasn't the answer
Food wasn't the answer
Shopping wasn't the answer
Minimalism wasn't the answer
Porn wasn't the answer
Channel surfing wasn't the answer
Video games weren't the answer

I have to journal

I have to tread in the suck
to learn to swim through it
or else I sink in the suck
and take years to undo it

And I'm running out of years

UNDONE

pardon me
as I peel off this toxic
positivity.
I'm a walking mood swing and
personality isn't real
so
the next time you ask how I'm doing –
I'll tell you how I've done so much doing
I've come undone
and hope you can point me in new directions to run

HOW TO SUCCEED AT MORNINGS

Please stop reading books about the brilliance of waking up at 5am
to cram those miserably healthy habits like nose breathing and raw
nutrition into one scrawny slot of freedom.
No one is looking, nothing is real, and none of this matters
anyway so if self-help feels like self-hell then go with your gut and
tell your soul that living with purpose is not this complicated but
you have to stop listening to friends or billionaires whose first
waking hour includes taking cold showers before hyper speeding
their way through today's to-do list.
Mornings require more PLAY, not more discipline,
so find a job to work in the afternoons and nights because all you
do between 1pm and 5pm is jerk off and all you do after dinner is
wonder about how boring you are.
Then take back the 260 mornings you annually give to a job that
pays you to flawlessly jaw your way through business cliches and
instead,
I don't know,
make cool shit that makes you go "oh shit, that's cool" –
throw vases, write riddles, draw butts, sing shanties.
My guess is you already know how you want your mornings to go
but you gotta break a few hearts to get there and one of those
hearts may be your own.

BLISS

obsessive and
unapologetic –
withhold your rhetoric about the benefit of balance,
let me drown in prepossession until I choke on
bliss,
when the banality of even-breathing regains its marketability.
meet me at the countdown of my collapse to capture a cataclysmic
blur,
a rapture most curious,
furious yet demure.
for when you see existence with such
pervading disinterest like me,
you'd climb each pique impulsively
or fossilize otherwise.
the options are polarizing
but symbolize an implicit equilibrium.
for all the moments of cycling through movements on tepid
treadmills of timidity, there exist kisses with such
explicit specificity to make the internet
blush.
and if you can reject your collection of inconsequential
momentum, then I can still fight, rightly – fist, tooth, and knife-ly,
and together we can drain the swamp of chagrin and
replenish the reservoir with serendipitous whims
and perpendicular sins
and je ne sais quoi...
but you gotta jut that chin up like you fucking mean it –
rise without rhythm
tighten that grip
turn to flex at the wreckage you've been until now
and breathe

TWO WEEKS NOTICE

Maybe I needed you to expose and break me
so that I could stand face to face with the fake me,
dispose of
and remake me

I'm not thanking you –
even though I'm an imposter
I still think you're an asshole

But I can thank the universe,
for merging our stories –
for showing me the only way to stay
was to play pretend
better than you

HOW TO STOP LYING (PART 1)

Stop talking.

Grow distant
Disappear
Isolate

Admit you're a
drifting
two-faced
coward

Rot
Rebuild
Resurface

Wear a warning sign
Let fewer people in

Don't make plans
Don't make promises
Don't explain feelings
Don't talk about the future

Go with your gut

THE RESISTANT DRIFTER

the resistant drifter
the mercurial mover
convinced of the virtue
to stay
reluctantly subscribes
to still.
suppresses
restlessness
with micro doses
of disassociation –
subsists on
malted shots of exalt
and pints of vanilla guile.
persists listlessly
through existing rites
committed as gist
honest as a grifter
shifting names
evading sight
until
the mercurial mover
embraces the
blissful volatility
of flight
and the resistant drifter
subscribes to a revised virtue
wherein
resistance is the villain
and the only sense of still
resides
in the drift

IRREDEEMABLE

The falsehood of adulthood
wants to reduce us to flesh bags of
repetition
but I am made of mud.
I reside in a stubborn persistence of malleability –
I am
irredeemably
filthy and
industrious.

THE FOOL

I am a fool
wholly committed
and fully declared
not subscribed to lifelong learning
but submitting to a lifestyle of
yearning –
for it's the
jarring
incompletions and
staggering
impermanence
that staves off deletion

And I have found
the most unsettling sounds
when I've settled in
and slowed down
being bound by the drift
is better than being drowned by it
so I move
neither fast nor furious
rather
drawn to the sudden shift
where I can be
unabashedly
brash and curious

I'm poisonous
in positions of
predictability
the weekly reload
of routines
the exhibitionism
of expertise
has always been the end of me
not the whole me
but the me you knew
the one we're both still trying to forget

the savior turned scum
more likely to abandon than commit to
best to run away from than into

I never meant to be the villain
I just get bored of being me
and I didn't know it enough then
to warn you appropriately
but I've hit reset
repeatedly
so much so the button sticks
so much so I'm stuck in a vile schtick
of burning down my completed lives
and digging through the ashes
to see who survives

But why stay alive
if I know how the story ends?
Why be more of what I've already been?
Then I'm a rerun
a replay of your most
masturbatory
moments in syndication
so I say
gimme your plot twists
gimme your anticipation
spit in your scripts
piss on your preface
take your soul by surprise
and succumb to new ways
to surrender yourself

I have to admit
that I can no longer predict myself
if I talk about the future
know it's a lie
if you can't close your ears
ready your sutures
because I never know
what I'll know tomorrow
and it's absurd of me to try
but if rewriting the story of me

has broken my promise to you
know that I'm still sorry for being so callow
know that I'm still sorry for when you saw me turn cruel
and that's why it feels right to call myself a coward
and that's why I commit now
to the ways of the fool

THE MARAUDERS OF MORASS
PART 1: INTRODUCTION

We are the cowards of tomorrow
Amok today
The marauders of morass
Hiding away

We settled in swamps
Away from the thrust of our lovers' trust
To commit to the marsh and the muck
We abandoned our plans for enchanting lands
To live in the sticks of the suck

We settled in swamps with swallowed scabs
And wounds as wide as seas
We festered in fogs and hovered the ground
To recover between the trees

We settled in swamps under covers of scum
Absconding with rum and pity
A gaggle of daggers and gathered guns
Incaved the teeth of our city

SWOON

Hmm, I guess the hardest part about dating in a world on fire while confronting its racist history during a pandemic is that people still like that old blood confidence as a sort of insurance for stability while everything else is off balance but that I don't have the traditional form of confidence where you can say something about yourself and it's still true an hour later...I'm more confident in how I tell you not to trust my projections because I don't know which of my hobbies will suddenly bottom out or spike in intensity, nor do I know how much longer I will want to live where I'm living, work how I'm working, be how I'm being. I am as definitive as a split infinitive, a fun but superfluous insertion that is more likely a distraction than an enhancement. Except I'm not really fun because fun is work and working hard or being on a couch and couching hard or looking at my phone and writing poems or doing anything that feels like I'm doing anything else than dying alone. I'm usually hungry. Do you like food? I'm usually horny. How about you? Lying down is nice. So maybe we can eat and fuck and sleep and talk about all of the impermanence that breathes through me and all the perversion that lives in you and when we get tired we can swoon and spoon in all those silly little ways that lovers do.

LET ME TRY

I'm so bored by being a consumer
and I'm tired of watching people
make good stuff sometimes but also
not-so-good stuff at other times.
I can do that.
Let me try.

THE LYING ALUMNI

the lying alumnus moves in a mercurial blur
among us today;
he's flying direct from a derelict boat in the
south of superior bay

we alumnae lie at the mouth of a river
remote from each other's stay
as the lying alumnus hides about in a tower
two miles away

in our crowd of laying alumnae sits the
sister of a slain alum;
her ashes lain in stainless steel with the
crest of a scorpio sun

we sprinkle her spirit surreptitiously
where the menominee river runs
to conceal the healing of her death,
revealing her vengeance has nearly begun

her form congeals to the sights of her
pisces rising to the task at hand,
coursing through mammoth rapids while
capsizing catamarans

limbs of the scorpio sun protrude from
her sides to intrude the land;
the gem of the lying alumnus cuts him in
two for the final stand

lunar twins split the skins of our slain
alumnae to four;
the flesh of our lying alumni chars as
archers ascend from his core

the alumnae summons tides to swamp the
fire igniting his pores
and wallop the lying alumni with waves to

whisk him to arctic shores

the lying alumni lies on the coast,
corroding from armor to bone.
the slain alumnae lowers her claws,
replacing her death with his own

his spirit resumes in lorusso lagoon,
her wraith is free to roam;
their shapes collapse in each other's laps
so neither decays alone

TRUST

if you meet someone with trust issues –
and they tell you a story where I am
the villain –
trust they're telling the truth
about a time when I didn't

I AM THE TRASH

my car is a trash can
and this one time my ex decided to look through
the center console and when I realized what was
at the bottom I said
holdonwaitaminutestopdigging
and she said why and I said you wouldn't believe what's in there
but it's condoms from when I slept with the girl my two best
friends were in love with and I didn't want to leave evidence of
our rendezvous so I hid the condoms in a spot they would never
look and then I moved for a job and the job got busy and then my
friends found out anyway and erased me from their lives so I
forgot about the condoms and then two years happened and now
you know the worst thing about me because my car is a trash can
and I am the trash

VOLATILE SCATTERSHOT

Nihilistic but smiley
Reliably tired
I heard you're absurd
Do you like to be choked?
I'll drink your words like whiskey and your cunt like coke.
Where do I sign up for the self-sabotage?
Take me to the ruins of a romantic mirage.
I'm just a phase.
I want to watch you jerk off and run away.
Put me in your footnotes
Stick me in your seams
A volatile scattershot of humanity and memes.
I LOVE YOU
  Nevermind
YES PLEASE
  Unsubscribe
Ignite
  Binge
    Burn
Never learn
Drown (
Me (
In (
Your (
Curves (
.Grab my ass.
"You can slap me harder than that"
Who am I? Who's asking?!
Who is anyone? Who cares?!
Let's eat cereal and watch cartoons.
Is it nap time yet?

SICK OF THE SUCK

I'm sick of the suck
and sitting in rust;
rudderless and twisted up
in wonder when's
and if then, what's –

I'm sick of the
slick of the wheel;
charting the distance
between my existence
and a corona commercial –

I'm
stuck in a glitch;
over encumbered.
More obsolete
than outdated –

I'm chipping away
at the daily hash;
carving up dark
counting down tallies
until I'm forgotten –

Until I can begin again

WHEN THE WORLD'S ON HOLD

what would you do
when the world's on hold?
would you grind and gut
to actualize your aspirations?
or would you drink and fuck
and down every drug you could?

how would you carry on
if you were a carrier,
a second-hand hitman with
invisible and undiscriminating
ammunition?

would you take any action
knowing any action could
expedite global demobilization –
strain supplies,
delay economies,
subtract civilization?

how far would you retreat…
how close would you play
your dread to your chest…
how much would you
withdraw your request
for human connection?

how would you react
when you uncover how
filthy or lonely or fake
or helpless or wrong
you've been this whole
time?

what amount of sedation do you
require between the
morning updates and nightly news?
how much of your messy little

existence can you supplant with
binges and books,
scrolls and smut?

how will you
press pause for the
foreseeable future,
knowing the future
is a new breed of
unforeseeable?

what will you do while the world's on hold?

THIS PIECE IS TRASH AND YOU SHOULDN'T READ IT
PART 3: SUSTAINABILITY IS MY PASSION

Nostalgia features a ranking system of desperation.
I graduated to a higher rank today when I started jerking off to a
movie I watched relentlessly 20 years ago called
Curse of the Catwoman.
I used to watch it on a VHS that I copied from another VHS that
I borrowed from the cousin of a neighbor of a friend because that
is how we used to live.
But now we have Pornhub, which has a search function,
which helps me hate myself less for throwing away my VHS of
Curse of the Catwoman 10 years ago.
But I can't shake the feeling that I'm virtually disappointing my
fellow citizens that I never see or hear or talk to during a time
when people need the internet for a redefined quality of life.
People are streaming to stay connected, to take classes,
to make a living, to make statements,
and all I can contribute are recycled orgasms.
I don't know – feels selfish.
Oh! Also,
if you find the movie
Debbie Does Dallas '99,
can you send me the link?

MY ONE GOAL

My one goal is to not get hit by a car.

It's a neat, demonstrative example of all those SMART goals I tried to teach people about in my twenties; Specific, Measurable, Attainable, Realistic, Time-Bound. But a singular goal is regularly challenged by context, and my context is the carrying of a personality which splits time between being a shut-in and a narcissist.

As a shut-in, when I eventually leave home, I am reminded that real cars exist, not just as machines in Vin Diesel flicks and video games; not just as a vessel I used to operate as part of my regular practice of living as a fellow human among the many who be, go, or drive to a temporarily meaningful destination.

After sitting inside for a week straight, I have to remind myself that cars are much bigger and faster than me. Is this what people thought when they first met the automobile? Instant humility? Automated fear? Walking across a street or through a parking lot feels like stepping onto a shooting range; the musculature of my neck stretches like a target, feeling the burn of a bounty materializing in the corners of concrete, the shine of windows.

Staying inside all day generates an irrational fear about what's "out there", but when my personality setting switches to narcissism, I should be more worried about the inner confusion of my universal importance. I can wake up on the right side of a mood swing with the belief that I'll out-joust a Ford F-150, survive a rush-hour stampede, dictate movement like a sign the neighborhood kids haven't stolen yet.

But cars don't have to stop for me. Cars may not see me physically or see me spiritually as significant as I believe the world should. Any car could jump a curb, and any driver could be an idiot or subscribe to moments of idiocy; I know this because I'm a member of both parties, the rare double agent with full loyalties to both sides.

I like having a goal though, especially an absolute one. You either are or are not getting hit by a car — no room for interpretation. I've grown tired of those other goals; the routines and schedules and habits. There're too many flaky negotiations and irregular calendars around the pursuit of stabilized excellence. Set it and regret it. My motivation now comes from asking *What hurts if you don't do it today?*

This is why I nap, to disrupt the exhaustive slog of prolonged consciousness. This is why I'm vegan, to protect my insides from the recklessness of my taste. This is why I go to the gym, because I've felt the pain of perpetual stillness, or worse, the psychotic jab of your only movement coming from a treadmill of anxious meanderings.

This is why not getting hit by a car is my trendy new resolution. It's simple, more motivated by preservation than evolution; find a way to keep existing until the time comes when you are ready to aspire for more than the absence of pain: A placeholder until you're ready to live for more than the avoidance of death. But until then, I have one goal, and most days I almost fuck that up too.

THE MARAUDERS OF MORASS
PART 2: THE CHORUS OF ROT

We are the cowards of tomorrow
Hidden today
The marauders of morass
Rotting away

We settled in swamps to warn our guests of
The swarming and steady unrest
We jilted all talk of decorum to wilt in the
Mud of slugs and pest

We settled in swamps in a smatter of smoke
And kept warm as our histories charred
We dug up the routes to the road we're told
Were best to let mold and discard

We settled in swamps and bayous of bluff
With walls of fog and twine
We rejected the calls of our basin to follow
The howls of swallowed time

TODAY

When I deleted Facebook after ten years and five states and six jobs and five hundred friends,
I didn't give a warning.
I wasn't running a social experiment as much as a spiritual one.
Reminiscing became impossible to resist and there existed too much evidence that I'd
Already lived
And all I had left to do was narrate my past;
incessantly and without solicitation.
I was every senior in the 6am McDonald's cafe,
at the precocious age of 32.
But I could never find a way to look back AND look forward (that's not how necks work)
and my self-control shows a history of insufficiency unless I mess around and get a little bit
nuclear.
When I deleted Facebook, I didn't delete my past but I learned about how re-living my past is an option and I'd rather not. And it doesn't really matter how many photos or friends I made along the way,
all I ever have is today.

NUMBERS

my one lesson from eight years of minimalism

stop counting –
owning more was never the answer before
just like how owning less isn't the answer now.
this isn't a numbers game.
instead,
when you are
unsettled,
can you address the source of your sorrow
without succumbing to distraction?
can you
breathe in the trials of silence
and exhale the reality that rattles you?
if yes, then go do it.
if no, quit your stereotypical shit, sit still, and
go through it.
that pain is just as impermanent as any smile you bore before.

yes, you probably have too many coffee cups
and those old socks are not going to renew their
elasticity;
but you can.
this isn't a numbers game.
this is about how your rituals wish to shield you
from the threat of shedding –
from the undoing of knowing who you are to
showing how unknowing you are.
but showing me how much or how little you
have just shows me how much your priorities remain
misplaced:
the fixation sustains on stories of stuff.
so sure, purge your space of excess, un-junk
your drawers, make another donation pile.
as long you remember that "less" is not a
prerequisite for becoming less broken.

stop counting
this was never a numbers game.

this was always about your tactics –
your subterranean interference with a series of
signals suggest that how things are
is no longer
how they can be.
maybe you were wrong in a big way.
maybe you were right all along but your rightness is too surprising
for you or the folx who claim to know you best and you may
have to choose between losing people and losing yourself.
maybe you feel so dead on the inside that starting over is the only
way to not feel dead on the outside.
stop counting.
or rather – start.
start counting the years you've committed to being a champion
for anyone else's spirit than your own. the rest of the math will
take care of itself.

REMEMBER

do you remember the time
we let go of our pasts
and committed to life
while it lasts?

do you remember when we stopped
resisting our want
because you called "adulting"
the failure's flaunt?

do you remember the warnings we gave?
"if you witness me boast about loyalty,
if you see me commit to a host,
run! or ready my grave –
for you've seen not me but a ghost"

HOW TO STOP LYING (PART 2)

use hyperbole in poetry not in conversation.
don't make to-do lists; if you wanted to do something you'd be
doing it now or you'll remember it later.
nostalgia = depression, not "I should do that again".
if old solutions worked you would not still have the same
problems and be trying to find new solutions in old solutions.
stop trying to connect with people if there is no connection; your
personality will activate automatically around the right ones.
"fake it 'til you make it" is the death sentence of identity. suck
hard until you suck less but don't lose you along the way.
if it's hard to explain, don't. some lessons don't translate into
words and the only one who needs to understand is you.
you can make plans but don't make conversations about making
plans.
talk about the work when it's done.
or don't. just keep working; you've said enough.
listen to your indecision –
unsure means no.
sure means no.
most things mean no.
follow the few that make you stir.
also, you should probably go to therapy.

MERGE

We know that this is a fake real
another remake of the unreal
but it may be
how we become
all of me
eventually
the elusive venue
in seeking synchronicity
replete with the cling
of clashing defenses
complete with conflicting sound
a bit of boardroom cacophony
on a part-time battleground

We know that this is helping
even if we bedazzle our moods
with hyperbole
or rush our waste
of time and space
impermanently
even if we dress too casually
or out-vogue the occasion
extravagantly
it feels like a boost in honesty
the gull to
gush through confessions
of the perverse
and frivolous
usher in the hurt
while overstating the oblivious

We know we need to be seen
so I guess I'll try the fake real
for the outside
instead of the real-real
where we hide
tightly sealed and
terrified

an unsightly show
of a tired disguise
that is so five years ago
a fashion craze
better off razed
than accessorized

We know we've been reserved
but it's time to manifest
the rest of us
assertively
to make
a passing impression
terminally
merge words
with actions
more congruent and true
more rightly aligned
with the flashes and signs
of the future me we're leaning into

We know nothing for sure
maybe I'm here to heal
or maybe we've already arrived
and all I needed for our grand reveal
was to burn out and stay alive

TWO

REPLACED

THE AWAKENING

Hello,

I'm you two years from now. I want to let you know that luxury
hotels and sex addiction are symptoms of your broken existence.
Oh, and you hate your career and the life you built around it and
the identity you've curated to match; you just don't know it yet.
That's ok,
the awakening is on its way.
That undercurrent of fear following you
and how you drag your consciousness through the dread of a
misplaced sense of purpose –
that's you dying and me taking over.
Don't worry,
we still watch Futurama
but the difference between me and you is that you think you can
control who we are supposed to be and I know that who we are
supposed to be
cannot not be controlled.
I still don't know if you are a complicated hero or if you're just an
asshole – I still don't have answers – but the sooner you let go, the
further we can move away from the feeling that you're going to
die an impostor.

Wimmy Wham Wham Wozzle,
The Other Joe Rolnicki

LOGICAL

I was a dreamer
until I convinced myself not to be;
seduced by the allure of security.
And I was secure enough to be successful
as a parallel me;
close,
but distant enough to be unsettling –
me,
but not me.
So twelve years later,
I'm dreaming big again
because that's far more logical
than dreaming small
which didn't feel much like dreaming at all.

SABOTAGE

Today feels like a day where I'll go to the bookstore and roam and buy a bunch of stuff I'll never read, which is what I did when I read voraciously but now that I read sporadically it sounds all the more like sabotage.

Still, I miss the calm reassurance of a slow day in a stacked room with towering spines and the smell of ink, like how a video store on the walk home from school let me sample their stories so I didn't have to admit to resisting my own. But video stores stopped existing and bookstores only persist as museums of missing out:
All I see now is the art I'm not making;
the inventions of minds who didn't waste their boredom and knew how to invest their restlessness.

So maybe I won't go today as a reminder that I've already seen the unremarkable life of the admirer. Maybe my legacy rests in the anxiety of this chocolate apollo chair so we'll sit.
And we'll wait.
And we'll remember why I'm not the guy who roams book stores anymore.

WHY NOT

New habits fail frequently.
my habits
specifically.
Habit stacks.
habit schedules.
tiny habits –
so atomic
I miss when they go missing

But I still try
to belt out
glossy-eyed,
semi-delusional
renditions of
hope;
hope that the
better version of
me is on the way.
Even if hope starts with
submission –
a reversal of decision

Impeaching the slumbering
perspicacious
leader of WHY
in favor of the
gun-slinging
madcap
boots-to-the-moon
executor of
WHY NOT

Why not
dare
to diminish
the rift between
who you are
and who you are

scared
you'll never be?

Why not
welcome
the burn
and the blisters
of a crude and
unfinished
formula?

Why not
mess up
your setup;
disinfect your
approaches
and distill
your know?

Why not
test if reality
has any commonality
with imagination
at its worst?

Why not?
A little hope never hurts

SECOND ADOLESCENCE

Don't mind me
just evaluating mortality
disguising my misery in misguided strategy

Go find me
just brandishing duality
wielding each mood as a new personality

Don't time me
just searching for purpose
lodging in mirages until it emerges

Don't mind me
just making a list
of all the times I got it right
and all the signs I missed

Go find me
just dripping retaliation
through a second adolescence to defy my station

Know I'm me
just reversing decisions
unearthing my worth without your permission

NEXT

My
Only
Goal
Is
To
Never
Know
What
I'll
Do
Next

SMOKY

I don't remember my dreams,
but you were there last night.
If I had to guess, you commandeered a horse-drawn rocket ship to
go ice skating on the rings of Pluto. You grew bored and
implored sordid leaders to draw their swords and then ignored
them into oblivion. When they drew conclusions, you drew your
saber to emasculate the musk of their illustrious dictator: a
crocodile who smiles at the trials of gators and caters to traitors in
a time of war -

But they've never heard your voice before...
the smoky chorus of your syllables, the perspicacity of your plea.
They weren't ready for how your radiance
eradicates
despair.

Neither was I.

Upon declaring instant peace,
the denizens ceased their reticence while you resumed the prance
of your cosmic glide.
The crocs advanced,
the gators chanced
to unite in stance for the Electric Slide.
Or maybe it was the Boot Scootin' Boogie?
I don't know.
I don't remember my dreams,
but you were there last night.

OVERLAP

A photographer
Met a cartographer
In a sublime cafe.
One showed a map,
The other, a snap
Captioned
"If our hearts overlap
We depart today"

CARRIED AWAY

Two strangers
in two unacquainted cars
rely on the same unlikely median
to move.
An abrupt intersection
where they intercept a sliver of each other's
numbness.
"Where are they going?" each says
and see each other say
and see each other's playful perplexity –
welcoming the wonder of a moment following
thousands of moments without.
A curious glance,
a smile ten percent wider than normal – it's all
just enough romance to get carried away.
"That'll do," they each say.
That'll do

THE MIGHTY MISS GLORIA MAY

You rescue runes from ancient moons
cratered with jaded hearts.
I balm the wounds of static Junes,
you tear supernovas apart.

I beguile in planetary afternoons,
you promote lagoons to sea.
You walk with a brash galactic poise while I gawk
at uncharted debris.

I croon at the sight of metallic typhoons
you shatter to shallow wakes.
You could splinter the sky with brass harpoons and
lasso Jurassic lakes.

I write about all of your sightings –
I sit in saloons to say,
"The lighthouse at night will show you the fight
of the Mighty Miss Gloria May."

DOMINO

how about a domino of juxtaposition?
an exhibition of dissimilar images in pristine position.
a glistening gather of views you'd rather watch on
loop than love and lose – news of you to cherish today
before you change and the cues decay.

how about a cascade of inquisition?
a weary interrogation of your indecision.
a mix of your most despicable schticks all in one
shot like a parlor trick – bits and flashes of former
fashions you'd dare not leave on display.

REBRANDED TARANTULA

We can't just catapult the caterpillar's name
Or boast the butterfly's obnoxious fame;
We're rebranding tarantulas with sleeker features
To defy the style of our creature's frame.

We'll make fresh takes on your favorite brands
By giving tarantulas relatable hands
And wrists to hold watches with silicone bands
To go with the glow of their golden tans.

We rebranded tarantulas for domestication
And hassle-free travel on your summer vacation.
We'll negotiate treaties with countless nations
For a Rebranded Tarantula radio station.

Subscribe to our rebranded mystery box
For a chance at a tarantula journal that locks!
You can write about nights on luxury yachts
Where you showed off your Rebranded Tarantula socks.

See exoskeletons on Peloton bikes
And segmented appendages on weekend hikes.
Find our channel and smash those likes
To watch stock of the Rebranded Tarantula spike.

To promote their woven organic silk
We worked with cage-free coconut milk.
It'll power you through the Tarantula Tilt,
The new dance craze on the app we built.

If you're the wanderlust type, we know how to reach you
So we sent our tarantula to Machu Pichu.
If you want to go bigger here's a Goliath Birdeater
In an old timey poster with a holstered repeater.

At Tarantula Ranch you can shriek away stress
As a colony cascades across your chest.
Our holistic retreats were voted BEST
By the Arachnid beats of the lower Midwest.

We've rustled up rivals at ADT
To provide your home with security.
Because who needs cameras accessed remote
When you install our Rebranded Tarantula moat?

In our collective effort to bring weaving back
We made the cover of SPUN with Fleetwood Mac.
And we travelled through time in an aggressive approach
To sling enough singles to squash Papa Roach.
You can learn about how all that hullabaloo went
By tuning into the Hulu exclusive event.

We've gathered the hair that juts from their pores
To mold a remarkable pompadour.
You can buy us on face masks and find us in stores,
The Rebranded Tarantula is finally yours.

LULL

If you call me for an interview,
prepare to hear about how
I didn't drink until my 34th
birthday and then became
a full-time bartender at 35
simply because I'd seen all of
life as a non-drinker and went
"fuck it,
what's it like on the other side?"
And you don't have to relate to
being so bored by your own
philosophies that you abandon
them for amusement but I hope you
are ready for me to
uproot
reality
during the afternoon lull
or out-pace the place
when the minutes crawl

RECKLESS

A cathedral rests on the bluff of a bay,
hesitating dilapidation.
We watch her pray for more tomorrows today
and await her collapse although she insists to stay.
A history of disregard for humanity's maximum capacity ruptures
her structure in a voluptuous way and the remedy of age sees her
settled for the better: The medal is mettled by weather, the wood
more grounded, as a whole – unfettered,
from foundation to sounds that bellow the clouds from her base
when it's time to sing
or when her silence astounds the pernicious wishes parishioners
attempt to bring.
She's bothered
but she doesn't brood like you;
she carries a poise that poisons with envy and
belittles with sophistication.
To dwindle
was never designed to appear so scintillating –
not to suggest that your brand of broken is unbecoming but
no one
makes *damaged* look this good.
And you wonder if you've ever stood with such
recklessness –
or if it's too late to start now,
or if now is the exact time to start,
like the cathedral that rests on the bluff of the bay,
not awaiting collapse nor time to elapse but
embracing the winds that pass each day.

ANYWAY

encourage your surface to immerse in urges
submit to a terse exchange
extend your thirst for the unrehearsed
accommodation of the strange
disdain your inhibitions
solicit disarray
the morning comes regardless for the heartless anyway

allay our indecision with
salacious
salutations
replace your worst
impurities
purge your meditations
bewitch us with
elixirs
cast me to the dirt
talk about forever while you render me inert

sway
with sagacity
misplace your inquisition
cure us with mercurial cascades of exhibition
then show me to the door
remove me from your chest
or
run away with me tonight and we'll figure out the rest

GOBLIN

I dressed like a goblin yesterday after not showering throughout a weekend where I ruined every lead on Tinder. I packed clothes worn by my last four renditions, hoping to trade them to a strip of vintage shops in a trendy neighborhood in downtown Austin. I made little eye contact, less conversation, and provided zero charm. I offered two and a half boxes and they bought a half of a half of a box because I am a monster and I wear dumb clothes.

And now I'm getting ready to dress more like a bartender who works out of a trendy shipping container in downtown Austin. I'll elicit more grins that grimaces and guests will smile with their teeth even if they're trying not to. I will turn heads and even inspire a few double takes.

And this duality of whether to goblin or not is another reason why I stopped making blanket statements about who I am. Personality is a channel – don't like what you're watching? Give it 30 minutes, see what's on next.

KEEP GOING

I keep doing new, weird things
And I need to keep going

QUEEN OF THE SLUGS

ACT 1: Wherein our Queen knows your motives
Queen of the slugs
Obscene in her magnanimity
Unforgiving in her
Gumption
For she suspects
The noble dregs
Who lush for her mantle
And permits the most obsequious leeches to
Beg but only to bequeath their
Unbecoming.
"Allow them to flummox and flush"
She says
But will never rush to reward a ward who
Doesn't blush enough for her prestige

ACT 2: Wherein our Queen cares not of your trifles
Queen of the slugs
Can catch your ballistics
Or snatch you in her mastery of
Ornate linguistics
"That crown isn't heavy at all"
She says
"If you wish to aggrandize the trials of men,
You should see my
Tuesday afternoon"

ACT 3: Wherein our Queen gets galactic
Queen of the slugs
Extinguished kings and diamond rings
Before terraforming the Sun
"If I can badge back badgers and shake down
Snakes, certainly I can say bollocks to the
Limits of mollusks –
You've never seen gastropod astronauts
Because you've never seen me
Uninterrupted,
But I'm too good for your dirt"

Says the Queen of the Sun,
Hearing pleas for her fire
Yet surrendering none

ALL OF THE ABOVE

7. None of this is real, nothing matters, and the world is ending so I might as well…

   A. Stop trying
   B. Transcend the implicit energy of all spaces and exist as an ethereal being of eternal love without the boundaries of self, ego, or expectation
   C. Manifest ruthlessly
   D. Start a ska band that exclusively covers Lady Gaga songs and call them Lady SkaGa

PARAPET

I walk
a pair of pants on a parapet aware that if my silhouette and spirit
met they'd share their fears for tears or sweat but forget the years
of barren threats from bludgeoning subconsciousness, muddying
self-confidence, plundering preponderance that everything I've
ever set my effort towards manifests something good or one thing
more than helplessness can barter for so bolt the doors to stories
told, chartered tours the snoring hold, bold the storms so waves
will fold our form for good or mold us more, like powering in
undertow by floundering in overflows of rogueing winds and
sunken husks and observances calamitous that test our stressed
agree-edness by repeating our retreated-ness, a blessed-be-thy
chorus set of how we've followed hollowed-beens and never-
dones but now I bet on just-for-fun-remember-whens and done-
it-once-but-not-agains, the wondrous magnificus of duncing
through the blunderbuss, succumbing to the calculus where
brazen best the cowardice, the lust for unencumbered must
outweighs delays of wonder-whats, the mold and rust will soon
combust so pull your trusty pair of pants to truss along the parapet,
dance and sing and better yet to live without a silhouette or talk as
vultures squawk for you –
assume the end will stalk in twos
take new heights before you balk
save your sky
and walk

DISSOLVE

Written with Clementine Valerie Black

quit talking and
let me dissolve
I'm not really a risk taker but the water in the pot
keeps boiling
and I wait for what comes next after nothing.
for now
it's a steady, gentle roar
unlike me
pants-less and slumped on the bathroom floor
(and we don't care about pasta anymore)
but maybe somewhere we do.
some rendition of us finds significance in the choice between
elbow and ravioli
tomato basil or basil alfredo
but here
you can boil any shape and simmer any sauce and just
throw it down our throats;
I promise it will taste the same because
(we don't care about pasta anymore)
nor pants
or floors, although -
it would be nice to care about something.
I'm not really a risk taker but here we are
still bleeding
waiting for what comes next after nothing.
it's a steady, gentle roar.
quit talking
let me
dissolve

GUEST

Tonight I see the skies yell electric in their rant against the roads.
Rancor flashes through my room as a reminder that
I'm only a guest here
and those morning birds and
soft breezes
exist not for my gentle awakening but
as a warning sign that there is no
definitive sound
for impending vengeance.
As our arena ages,
the sun sends me death threats through her rays and
I feel her disapproval when I select shelter from her
shine.
We both know of the burden I bring so I wait
for her to erode my form with a gauntlet of
unsuspecting scenery –
a bolt or
a gust or
an "it's so hot you can fry flesh on the sidewalk" sort of
arrangement.
I'm only a guest here
and soon my invitation will be
revoked.

REPLACED

I stroll through my gallery and see a series of
failed photoshoots with a stranger –
unrecognizable in his
unconvincing attempts to imitate a candid grin
and carry a counterfeit poise.
A prototype of miscalculations:

he knows this is not what the planets planned for
when they aligned.

But he doesn't know what I know yet,
so I laugh with a similar, spirited arrogance as the
person who will look through my gallery and see
me as a stranger one month from now.
And he'll have the same thought collapsing
my chest –

How many times have I been replaced?

THE MARAUDERS OF MORASS
PART 3: THE CHORUS OF HOPE

We are the cowards of tomorrow
Rotting today
The marauders of morass
Resisting decay

We settled in swamps and calming slogs
To drift as beasts of bones.
Bound to forage and feast through bogs
Where streams retreat to stones

We settled in swamps and damp encampments
Befitting a coward or two
We glittered our gilded abode with enchantments
And trappings to ease the view

We settled in swamps and sung along
To the song of swinging tides
We readied our mettle like soggy meadows
And soil waiting for sky

THREE

FREE TIME

FREE TIME

Give me enough free time and
I will reinvent what it means
to disappear –
now you see me,
now you won't
recover from how
I've corrupted your
assumptions;
and while you were busy
drawing conclusions,
I was busy colluding with
your predictability

Give me enough me time and
I will pioneer a new duality
as a reminder that
personality is a myth –
I am either alone in a room
or a mirror of you;
not a vessel in a vacuum but
a mass of
situational
creations
and my only permanence is
the surety of
impending permutations

Give me enough of a lifetime and
I'll give you the range
of a sobering soul
seeking strange;
rearranging aims
and lexical styles,
dissociating for days to levee the spirals,
donning opposition
and igniting trials
so the cemetery of me will green for miles.

We are a pile of plots,
a stack of stories.

I'm a transcript in stitches;
an allegory

LOU LEE (OF SAULT STE. MARIE)

No, I don't know that name no more.
Now they call me Lou Lee of Sault Ste. Marie –
I'm a Munising Man,
Where the Islands are Grand
And the tides romance you to stay.
I own a small home on a tall spot of land
In a town as blue as the bay

I play baritone sax in a traveling band
And refurbish furniture with tools on hand.
I speak with my silence and fight where I stand.
I own a 15-year-old frying pan

I shop at the local trading post
For crafted provisions unmatched by most.
I walk with my shoulders and dance with my feet
And say hi to the people I pass in the street

I sip coffee at dawn and down bourbon at dusk –
I groom blisters between the dark.
I paint with saws 'til I'm covered in dust and
My skin can chisel bark

Meet me at streetlights as soon as you rise,
I'll sweep heaps for the needs of your day.
Then hear my voice over radio waves
As you close on the coastal skies

I'm Lou Lee of Sault Ste. Marie:
I don't know of those names that follow me,
I drown old ghosts each day at sea
And that's why here is where I'll be

35

Today I turn 35 and I'm only alive because I keep dying
and being reincarnated as me, which would explain the
familiarity but it doesn't explain the
daring
or the discontinuation of caring or the freedom from
comparison or the short-term memory.
Today I turn 35 regardless if you're watching or if you'll
even remember me, and you can blame Astrology
or my Moon in Aquarius or my Gemini Sun or Rising
Sagittarius, but I only want to wake when I
don't know what's next –
beyond the fight for realignment
behind the signs to obsess.
Today I turn 35 as a reminder that
it's ok to not know about tomorrow,
it's ok to be unsure about today
it's ok to crash land without priorities or plans and
still be alive anyway.

AN INVITATION

I'm here now
In a way I never have been
And my worry is to be stirred with such disquietude that I roll up
in a moment so unknowing and cannonball my way back into the
purgatory of order and trendy deterioration adorned with
treadmill desks and dual monitors, designer manilla folder holders,
a small cork board clogged with slobbery thank you cards that
were probably mandatory anyway.
My new order is more disorderly and resembles an invitation to
the old, outmoded motions captured and cataloged across
centuries of expression; movements which stir with such fervent
continuity to make us dance and sing and write and drink and
fuck until the act of being tires us with such little mercy that we
must retreat to slumber in order to re-up and relentlessly spend
the next day's givings. But we stick the motion in a corner and
call it creativity – we call it art; categorized as superfluous and
specialized when it's more akin to sleeping and breathing, as if we
are not all movers but too disenchanted and static.
And I've been there, wanting yet awaiting
assignment...but I was never told to breathe or sleep and
I've always done and sucked at both so
I'm here now
In a way I never have been before
And I realize my worry is to see how many of us are still awaiting
an invitation

RULES

The best part of poetry is the bit about rules.
You want some? We got Sonnets and Haiku.
You want none? We got Free Verse too.
Otherwise,
All we need is you.
So let's get started.

THRASH

If you must know,
I want to thrash my voice with a throaty acapella
then nurse my cords in a cocktail of gravel and
kerosene.
I want to subvert your inhibitions through lawless
renditions of top ten hits on a rusty trombone.
I want to pluck at strings with enough abandon to
shred identity –
and let my
ripped tips
blister to blood and
drip
and drop bits of bone.
I want to dance
like everyone is watching
and getting their goddamn money's worth.
If you must know,
I've been delegated to the dirt
but I
am meant for the stage.

SOUND BARRIER

Charter a ferry or
merry-go-round
to the heart of a merrier town
so I can walk through the barriers of sound with you
and compose a prose
that shows I care how the marriage of sound
surrounds you.
Consider the whip of your tongue –
how it collects
quixotic selections
to slip through your lips
without election;
erect melodic connections to swerve
to the rhythm that has begun.
Honor the shape of your mouth –
how it moves
through ruins of sonic
conclusions
and renews without tiring
out.

What fashions of flush will
rush to your cheeks when the nouns
grow weak but the verbiage
piques? Is it the red of
brick
or the hue of rose or the gush that flows
when you catch a prick?
Have you seen when a rhyme
delays?
How a shiny rhapsodic
collection of expedited
expressions
captures your time 'til the rhyme returns
to align in delightful
ways?
And don't say you'll love me today
if you won't croon through a tune

of the oceans and moon
without drowning me in cliche.

Woo me with clues of
linguistic mystery and save your
rituals for dawn.
Fawn over me
idiosyncratically
before declaring I move along.
Oh my provisioner
of revisionist
history,
imprison me to your canvas and
canopy
or to the corner where I belong.
Hear ye!
Hear ye!
I decree
to be a flesh-bag of dreck and ecstasy.
And let's agree
to call this off
right before the end though
to say we touched the sky enough
to call you my
crescendo.

THE GOSPEL ACCORDING TO FOGHAT

I was driving when a song with a
killer guitar riff came on,
so I sped up

but the lyrics were:
slow ride
take it easy

so I touched the brake
slowed my ride
took it easy

but then the guitar happened again and I drove faster

and I just want to say how unprepared I was to be so
spiritually conflicted for eight minutes and seventeen seconds

SLAPSTICK

To the driver behind me –
I'm rollin' 10 miles below the speed limit because I have a
habit of buying cars that rattle when I push 60 and I
can't
un-visualize
the totality of my car's parts coming entirely undone at
70,
thus projectile birthing out a slapstick amalgamation of
me bobsledding down I 35
in a rogue driver's seat
with a loyal steering wheel
past a trail of sparks fit only for the fourth of July.
So unless you want to see my rendition of
Buster Keaton Meets The Dark Knight Rises,
change lanes
and just let me be bad at driving.

BLANCHE RISING

I've only seen one season of the Golden Girls and I'm still newer to Astrology but I'm most certainly a Blanche Rising with my Moon sign in Sophia and my Sun sign residing in a shared house on Miami Beach with a few other souls telling Death that we're not ready yet.

BIG TALK

If you don't like small talk
then ready yourself for
big talk
about you've never met
me
because my persona is the
greatest hits
of semi-successful
situational scripts
and any deviation is a cosmic glitch.
What else am I to do with all this
flesh?
I've wrecked
the curriculum of the living
and I wasn't raised to be an
aberration
but every time I choose strange,
I find peace,
even if I'm lost for purpose.
Why am I permitted continued existence
if not to subsist on
dance
& working hard &
fucking harder
because the world is ending so we might
as well finish it off as beasts and let go of
all this pesky self-consciousness.
Or,
if all that's too much -
this weather has been crazy lately,
amiright?

FARMER

At work I met a maker of rum from Poland.
I told her of my Polish lineage and
she said my last name means
farmer.
"I didn't know it meant anything"
I said
with a curiosity of how I'm allowed to exist for 30 years with a
non-existing awareness of heritage.
And I asked the maker of rum what else she could reveal about
my identity and she called on
optimism.
In my buttoned-up vest and
on-the-clock disposition,
I yammed on about my debilitating stretch of nihilism,
how I'm trying to manifest as a symbol of eternal love while
getting stuck in the suck of existential futility and she said
"Of course. That is
deeply Polish of you"
and stared past the entirety of my guile.
"Take me to our home and tell me more"
I nearly said.
"Show me who I am so that I might learn who I am to become."
But I had guests to attend to
and she had an empire to run.
We rushed out pleasantries and parted at once;
an oblivious farmer,
a maker of rum.

THE MARAUDERS OF MORASS
PART 4: CONCLUSION

We are the cowards of tomorrow
In a state of decay
The marauders of morass
Still alive anyway

Dying as liars but surviving the day
By igniting the fires we smothered to gray

And we settled in swamps
But we're not here to stay
The marauders of morass
Moving away

RASCAL

The truth is I've concluded my research and
I no longer wish to be a
sad boy.
I just want to be a
CONSTANT
fuck-up
and wreak havoc on my biography.
I want to read about my late thirties and gasp
"Wow,
How menacing?
What a rascal!"

SHOPPING SPREE/FASHION SHOW

Shopping Spree!
Looking for something to match my
Vanity
I'm over woe is me
So tedious
Taking this all so seriously
Build me a wardrobe you'd decry as
Deplorable
But maintain the sense that I'm frankly
Adorable
Fashion show!
Dress me in your most
Reprehensible
Brazen
Yet affordable
Emblazon me in gold
Go bold at the seams
Make me irredeemable
In ensembles that SCREAM
"Love me or
Fuck you"
And I'll take two
And then a dozen more
…
Maybe it's best I buy out the store

A NEW ERA

You may admire my aesthetic
but what do you think of
my collective reckoning?
The breakneck dissociation from arrested
development and the fawning
over a new era of
lust

NICE TO MEET YOU

after we met, I pictured my hand
wrapped around your throat – how you'd
close your eyes and beg for
pressure. I thought of you
crawling my figure,
positioning;
preying
       and pawing
             and slithering.
I want to watch you
thrash
       and brand me with your claws.
let me plead
to move for you. fill my pores
with your sweat.
stick your taste in me. make me
breathe the air
that doesn't deserve you anymore.
the pleasure's all mine.

SMIRK

Not looking for a good Christian gal
More in the market for a wrist-slittin' gal
Someone to spit in my teeth
Straddle my face to make me meek
And smirk as I struggle beneath

VULGAR VIK

Vulgar Vik
lived to suck cunt and eat dick
betwixt fixing elixirs and remixing
limericks.
The grand ambassador of
fishnet lipstick,
a wunderkind runner-up but always up and
cumming.
Vik commands each day as the lone colonial ponytail
in the back alleyway,
whose incorruptible brand is to ruin you and your rally
whole handedly.
"I will reduce you to rubble then
return you to Earth
before demanding you beg to earn your worth,"
sneers the Sultan of Sleaze.
Vik evokes mass proposals most casually
only to bellow
"oh hell no!"
with unshakeable ease.
Vulgar is the lemon-squeezed
salt deposit
on your festering knees, and a pundit in
interrogation.
"Sit still for me baby,
so I can probe your temptation to advance
the rancid monotony of modern
monogamy"

Vulgar Vik
wakes from wet sheets to take bets on boozing streaks.
Dime less,
lawlessly unwashed yet
unflawed by time,
as fine as old-world wines dumped in a trough and slurped by
swine.
A hapless,
haphazard attraction –

a strapped-on champion of assless chaps,
perfect for insertion or
impaling back.
"Didn't peg me as bottom-y?
I'll be more impressed with your sodomy when you invest in
my dichotomy"
-To rail or be railed-
Vulgar gags,
THAT! Is the question,
but is more likely to stroke spear than
Shakespeare
or allure you to inhale and smoke spears to make theirs
disappear.
"I'm cutting off cuffing season and claiming it fluffing season.
Tell me you love me with the back of your throat."

Vulgar Vik
indulges in bulges
then drags you to shows
with the dregs and the hags no one knows.
A showcase of brass knuckles and corresponding
belt buckles; a fit from toe to teeth. "If you seek
visual rituals -
look away,
but come with me to reverse decay,"
says the chaperone to the church of the
churlish, with congregations of nightcrawlers and
back-alley brawlers, through communions of rum and musk.
"Come one, Come all -
But me first"
Vulgar bursts.
"Has it occurred to your vacant incantations"
Vik will spout from their wayward station,
"That you can charge hard through head falls
and margin calls or
you can whimsically rescind the curse of chagrin
with the insistence to chase cigars with gin.
If we're not winning,"
Vik grins,
"Let's saddle up and get sinning,"
says the concrete critter.
The spiritual plunder,

who'll unholster your soul and tear your cares
asunder.
And you'll wonder if your plot has been as raw
or thick
before your eyes coincided with
Vulgar Vik

WEREWOLF ASTRONAUTS

I tried writing you a romantic
poem with the moon and the
stars but it just ended up being
about werewolf astronauts
doin' it

HEDONISM

Has daily life turned your genitals dry and
unbiased?

Do you worry too much about people,
and the things people are doing in places?
Well, isn't it about time you and your dumb hair
do something about it?

Try Hedonism

With hedonism you can choose to
subdue consciousness through our curated
selections of drugs, booze, and smut from
the country's leading experts.
You can even mix them together in our monthly
Bender Box,
shipped directly to the darkest corner of what you
claim to be home.
And if our goods leave you unsatisfied...
Buy more!
We have a strict no-refunds policy,
and an even stricter yes re-funs policy.
We all know this is the closest you'll come to
Happiness, so why wait?!
Try Hedonism today!

ABRUPT

These days are a
stiff reawakening
a big black dildo smack to the face right as I find my stride
closed eyes
at the behest of rhythms wishing to mesmerize my motion

These nights are a
crowbar to bedrock
gallivanting through dance floor aftershocks
in rooftop pools
and ghostly karaoke clubs

These times are
barbed and wired
riding sidecar
to dive bars and Thai cuisine
between sing-alongs to Santeria
and Stronger
where strangers belt range until they're strange no longer

These ways are a
dismissal of indecision –
submissions to whims and intuition,
where we sashay through
doorways
and staircases hidden
behind abrupt interruptions
to inhibition

LUSH

It is the day after the night before
and you can find me in the trees,
colloquial and shrill
in the pause between the breeze.
"Where the dang is my quill?"
I ask the villainized weeds
but the idle green is mum and un-aiding.
I *Balderdash* at the sun,
and reconsider literature
before recalling the appalling prerequisite of
loyalty.
I recline in the stand,
unready to dedicate dread to rhetoric but
submit to subliminal trysts with
affectation.
"I must slow
and grow as the greenery,
lumbering yet lush,
and slumber until my condition resumes the
constitution of the wicked"

MORE

wondering what good all my wandering is for
if all I'm ever moving towards
is a life of moving more

QUICKSAND

The quicksand shifts,
unhitching limbs from ephemeral spells and
crass attachments,
soon to re-concretize and
stick my silhouette in
a puzzling yet nostalgic
formation;
an uninvited sloshing of
unrequited restorations–
repositioning
from the flaunt of what I
had
to a want of what is
missing

MODERATION

I recently learned about a practice called
moderation
which suggests that we do not have to live
in extremes so instead of deleting Instagram
I just removed it from my phone and waited
ten days for my nervous system to regain its
composure
and I never wanted to be good at Instagram –
I only wanted to be good at becoming me
but I need to become me faster and I can't
do that if I constantly wonder if people are
engaging in my becoming or if they are
too busy manifesting themselves because
we're all wounded and out of whack and
attempting to realign our wackness in
public verse.
And I hope we can still emerge and fire
emoji together but this hot mess is starting
to boil and I've got to find an immoderate
way to simmer my ass down.

YOUR NEW SELF-CARE ROUTINE

The streets told me you were looking for a new self-care routine so I stole all the clocks from your bungalow and punted them north. I deleted your name from the global database so you may brandish anonymity until you start anew wearing any title you choose. I painted murals of goats and lighthouses in your sleep square, and the Bob's Burgers marathon is set to start any second now. I curated a charcuterie log and left a spread of dippable foods with a sea of sauces on a steam-powered coffee table that hovers bedside while shushing out a soothing tenor. I carved a hole in your weighted blanket to get you some of that fine leg air while the rest of you nestles as a burrito. I replaced each one of your pillows with two pillows because your pillow game is weak and one of us has to care about your reputation. If you have a comatose fever dream where the food starts to dip you or the pillows go to war, that's perfectly natural but maybe start practicing some de-escalation techniques now. I upgraded your smart phone to a cassette Walkman playing the Lion King soundtrack and you don't even have to flip the tape over because I pioneered technology that automates this action for you. I heard you were looking for a new self-care routine but you can stop looking because I found you first.

ANONYMOUS

Let's get anonymous
and swallow this city whole
Let us be phantoms
evanescent
ephemeral
Let's get taxonomous
then discard discriminations
Let us be truants who circumvent stipulations
Let's get negligent
and find fences to climb
Let us rule the world
one last time

DISTANT

Permit me
to be smitten
for just a little bit more

I'll keep my distance

but I'd rather not resist you when you're at the door

THE ONLY LOVE SONG
I'LL EVER NEED

The only love song I'll ever need is that Starship track from the movie Mannequin. I thought that at 8 years old while playing with Matchbox Cars and watching Kim Kattrall bedazzle Andrew McCarthy, I thought that at 28 seeing Bill Hader lip sync his way back into Kristen Wiig's good graces, and I thought that today drinking a Mexican Martini alone in an empty bar on a Wednesday afternoon in Lakeway Texas.
It bellows like the renegade anthem for old romance. Maybe I'm amazed at how I still gush over invasive whispers of a renaissance. Such a nice surprise,
me and my little old soul – crooning through a chorus about how nothing's gonna stop us now,
even when everything has.

SALSA TALKING

This might be the salsa talking but the view of your face is just the greatest and I hate to face how I'll ever replace it

HALL WAYS

my walls
looked best
with you pressed
against them

my halls
miss
the ways
of your walk

my floors
look drab
without your
fashion

my pillows
miss
your
talk

PROGRESS REPORT IN THE SEARCH FOR PURPOSE

And yet I must conclude that my purpose will
remain hidden without the weekly exchange of
hard work,
great sex,
poor sleep,
and unending self-exploration –
this intersection of four forces is where I sense lies the
requisite recklessness,
calm, and confidence to seek the meaning of an agency
untouched by the want of parenthood and
uncolored by the structure of Gods

TO THE CHILD I'LL NEVER HAVE

Suicide is an option at any age but so is reinvention. I don't know what your question is but somehow "ska music" is the answer. People don't care about how you dress or wear your hair so go find your style and be loud about it. Dawn of the Dead (1978) is better than Dawn of the Dead (2004) but stay open to new perspectives. If our planet still twists and you shake off my debilitating nihilism, please fight for feminism, Black Lives Matter, trans rights, anti-racism, upending white supremacy, castrating the patriarchy, and decapitating capitalism. Like or love or sleep with whoever you want but let's talk about consent and polyamory. Personality isn't real - allow people and places to pull out versions of you that are unrecognizable. Life is short but it's also way too long. We're not great at desk jobs. Having to make money is dumb but so is being a mid-level manager so just get by and go art. You may be somewhat skilled at every sport because we all are. You'll grow into your nose or your hair or whatever part of you that feels like a caricature at 13. You won't care for religion (none of us do) and astrology is too cool and eerie to ignore. You get one big dumb lump of time so don't be who they want you to be - they don't even want to be that.

TIMELINE

I don't keep a bucket list but I have recurring visualizations
which I'll casually earmark as
destiny.
They are "part of my timeline," I'll say.

My timeline is the reason I'm choosing to stay alive even though
it feels like my story is complete.
I sit like a tired child in the backseat,
groaning through dramatic renditions of "are we done yet?"
while Destiny says "nuh-uh, we're Just. Getting. Started"
and blasts radio edit Black Eyed Peas while I sulk in waiting.

My timeline is why I became a bartender at 35 and got a tattoo
sleeve at 34.
It's why I left my first career at 33 and committed to ethical non-
monogamy at 31.
I knew these projections were more than whims or what ifs,
they were doors that would unlock the next part of my story.

Like, at some point in my timeline, I'm supposed to
fall in love with a sex worker,
work in porn,
become a jewelry guy,
face a serious addiction,
work in Vegas,
amass an empire of goats,
live on an island,
retire to the water,
and die as a local in a lake town.

Also,
I think my brother and I are supposed to live together again and
start a family business in a line of work our family has never done
business before.

I don't keep a bucket list but at least I see flashes of a future where
there used to be none, so I guess the rest of my story is far from
done.

STORM

I stopped looking for warning signs once I realized that
I am the storm
and I'm already here

ACKNOWLEDGMENTS

I don't believe my Father or my Mother has read any of my writing, but like all other lifestyle shifts I've made over the years, they've supported the spirit of my efforts from the beginning. I can't overlook the compassion necessary for parents to endorse their child jumping off a corporate ladder to write poetry and make cocktails; this book doesn't happen without them.

I met Steven Hugh Nelson in high school, and we always talked about doing big creative projects together but never truly acted on it until we moved in together in 2019. Our aspirations pulled us in different directions, but I had my writing renaissance at the same time he committed to working in horror movies, and I believe our prioritization of creativity helped fuel each other's focus on being makers more than consumers. He is the only person I asked to read my pieces when I doubled down on writing and he is the first person I told about this book becoming a reality.

When I started posting pieces to Instagram, I found a small community of writers who helped me continue to play with the range of writing through prompts and collaborations. I co-wrote two mirror pieces, including *The Only Love Song I'll Ever Need*, with my favorite writer, Ellie Sparks (@justtryingtobeoriginal). I co-wrote one of my favorite pieces, *Dissolve,* with Clementine Valerie Black (@clementinevalerieblack), and her prompts helped me complete two other pieces, *Reckless* and *Domino*. Speaking of prompts, *The Mighty Miss Gloria May* would not have found its final form without the prompts from Mae Rose Finnigan (@maerosefinnigan), *An Invitation* would not exist without a prompt by T.S. Priest (@agirlcalledthomas), and *Queen of the Slugs* only manifested when K.L. Pezzutto (@klpezzauttoauthor) referred to herself as such in one of her stories; I loved the title so much I started writing the piece immediately. I treasure those bits of serendipity.

Several of my fellow Instagram writers agreed to read an early copy of the manuscript and provide reviews in less than two weeks' time, and I'm grateful for the diligence in their efforts and the kindness in their words.

In early 2021, I fell into an unexpected romance with a lady who immediately became my muse. She is the inspiration for *Smoky*, *Distant*, *Salsa Talking*, *Anonymous*, and more.

All of the folx at Atmosphere Press helped me turn this pile of pieces into a story of poems with a gorgeous cover, and I would rather not think about how unpolished this whole volume would be without their guidance.

And finally, I want to acknowledge Joshua Fields Milburn, known mostly for his being one-half of the Minimalists along with Ryan Nicodemus. Their writings helped me turn my consumer-focused lifestyle around in 2013, and when I decided to pursue writing in 2019, it was the online writing class of Milburn that helped me discover poetry as my favorite form. Milburn was central to the two most significant windows in my adulthood, and his writing continues to help guide me even now as I've started making my way through the newest book from The Minimalists.

ABOUT ATMOSPHERE PRESS

Atmosphere Press is an independent, full-service publisher for excellent books in all genres and for all audiences. Learn more about what we do at atmospherepress.com.

We encourage you to check out some of Atmosphere's latest releases, which are available at Amazon.com and via order from your local bookstore:

I Would Tell You a Secret, poetry by Hayden Dansky

Aegis of Waves, poetry by Elder Gideon

Footnotes for a New Universe, by Richard A. Jones

Streetscapes, poetry by Martin Jon Porter

Feast, poetry by Alexandra Antonopoulos

River, Run! poetry by Caitlin Jackson

Poems for the Asylum, poetry by Daniel J. Lutz

Licorice, poetry by Liz Bruno

Etching the Ghost, poetry by Cathleen Cohen

Spindrift, poetry by Laurence W. Thomas

A Glorious Poetic Rage, poetry by Elmo Shade

Numbered Like the Psalms, poetry by Catharine Phillips

Verses of Drought, poetry by Gregory Broadbent

Canine in the Promised Land, poetry by Philip J. Kowalski

PushBack, poetry by Richard L. Rose

Modern Constellations, poetry by Kendall Nichols

Whirl Away Girl, poetry by Tricia Johnson

ABOUT THE AUTHOR

Joe Rolnicki graduated from Moraine Valley Community College and Dominican University before attaining a Masters of Science in Education from Northern Illinois University. After leaving his first career in 2019, Joe abandoned the genres of emails and training manuals to pursue creative writing options, his early favorite being poetry. Joe grew up in the Midwest but currently resides in Austin, Texas. *Second Adolescence* is his first book.

To connect with Joe, visit joerolnicki.com or follow @theotherjoerolnicki on Instagram.

Printed in Great Britain
by Amazon

78861310R00073